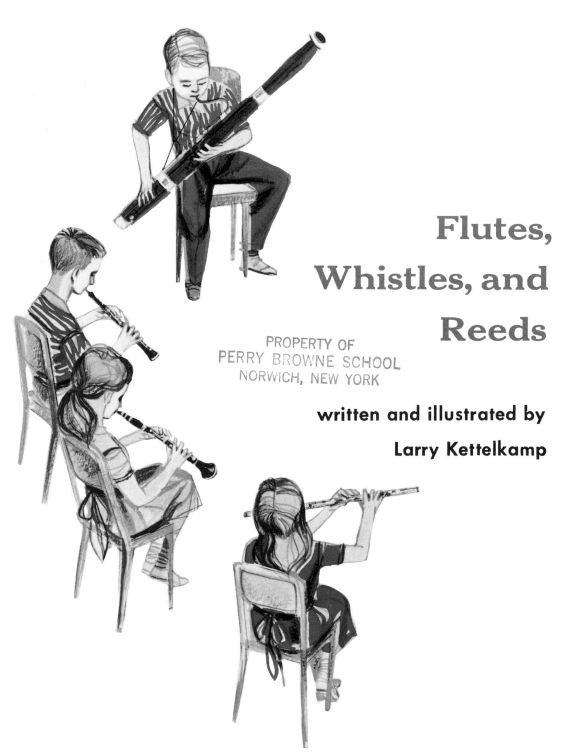

Flutes,
Whistles, and
Reeds

written and illustrated by

Larry Kettelkamp

WILLIAM MORROW AND COMPANY, 1962

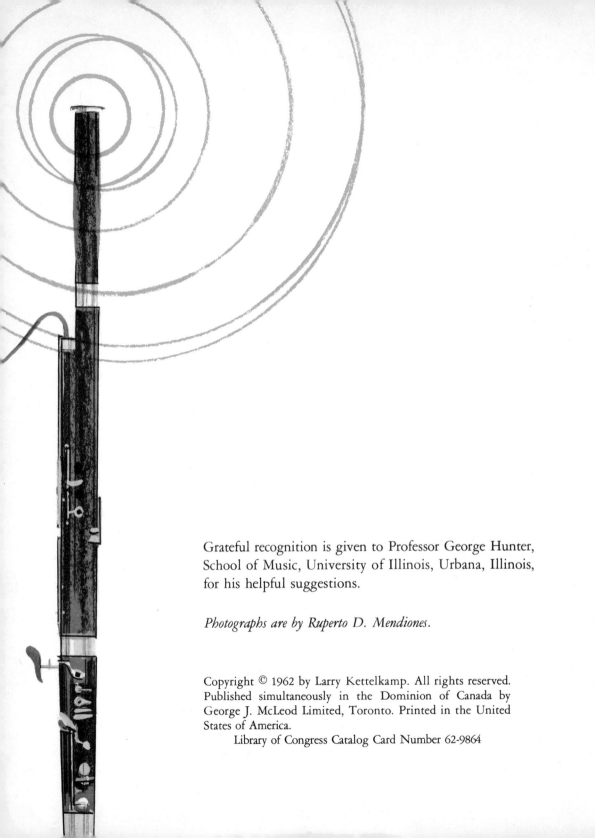

Grateful recognition is given to Professor George Hunter,
School of Music, University of Illinois, Urbana, Illinois,
for his helpful suggestions.

Photographs are by Ruperto D. Mendiones.

The Woodwinds

Anything hollow holds air. If you set the air inside a hollow object into regular motion, you will hear a pleasant sound. This is how the music of a group of instruments called the woodwinds is made.

These instruments are hollow, and many of them are made of wood. The flute family and the reed family of instruments belong in the woodwind group. The sounds of a pipe organ are also made in the same way, so it, too, is related to this group.

When a player blows into a flute, the breath stream itself vibrates. If he blows into a reed instrument, his breath causes one or two thin cane reeds in the mouth-

piece to vibrate. In either kind of instrument the air inside it picks up the vibrations and makes rich sounds, such as those we hear when a flute, oboe, clarinet, or bassoon is played.

Modern woodwind instruments developed from such simple sound makers as plant-stem whistles, bamboo shepherd's pipes, and willow-bark reeds. You can make these simple instruments for less than a dollar plus your own patience and care. The only tools you need are a pocket-knife, a coping saw, a pair of scissors, a file, and a vise. Those you build and play will help you understand why woodwinds work as they do and how men learned to make beautiful sounds from them.

Whistling Flutes

If you blow across a hole in a hollow object, you will make a sound. You can sound a piece of bamboo just as you can an empty pop bottle. If you blow across the end of a fountain-pen cap, it will give a shrill tone. If you blow across a hole in the side of a dried gourd, it will give a mellow sound. Even your own mouth sounds when you whistle.

In much the same way all of the instruments in the flute family make sounds. A stream of air strikes a sharp edge of the instrument. The stream splits—some goes outside and some goes inside. The splitting air stream jiggles, or vibrates, and starts the air inside vibrating. In some flutes, the player's breath blows directly against an edge. In others his breath enters a built-in tube, which aims it against an edge in a narrow stream.

5

The pitch you hear depends on how much air the instrument contains. Smaller or shorter instruments hold less air, which vibrates more frequently and gives higher pitches. Larger or longer instruments hold more air, which vibrates less frequently and gives lower pitches. The kind, or color, of the sound you hear depends on what the instrument is made of and what special shape it has.

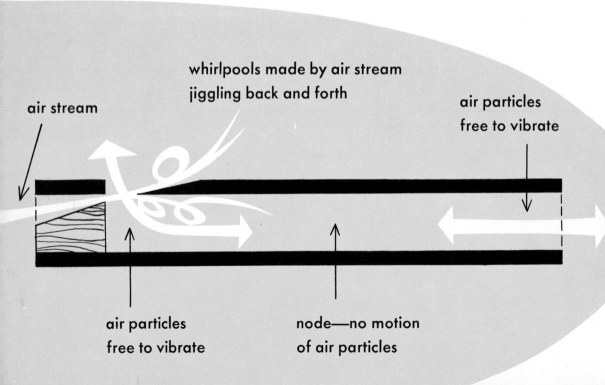

whirlpools made by air stream jiggling back and forth

air stream

air particles free to vibrate

air particles free to vibrate

node—no motion of air particles

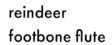

Chinese "goose egg" and
modern ocarina, both of
baked clay

The First Flutes

Flutes made of hollow reindeer foot bones have been found that are tens of thousands of years old. As these bones dry out they become hollow, and blowing holes can be cut in them. Other natural hollow objects, such as an ostrich quill or a dry gourd, were also used as simple flutes. Later pots and jars of oven-baked clay were sometimes used to make good flutes.

Hollow bamboo was one of the best

ostrich
quill
whistle

7

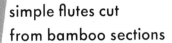

flute materials. Bamboo open at both ends is called an open tube. Bamboo open at one end and closed at the other is called a closed tube. The air inside an open tube vibrates at both ends. The air in the middle is trapped at a dead spot called a *node.* Thus the air vibrates in two equal sections. If one end of the tube is closed off, the node is then at the closed end rather than in the middle. The whole column of air vibrates instead of the two halves. The pitch of the closed tube is about one octave, or one do-re-mi scale, lower than that of the open tube of the same length.

Because of this principle, a bamboo flute player could play two different notes by covering and uncovering the end of the tube with one hand as he blew. When he covered the end, he made a closed tube

8

Bamboo flute players make tunes by opening and closing tubes and also blowing overtones.

open tube

node

closed tube—
an octave lower

node

open tube—same pitch as half-length closed tube

closed tube—an octave lower

node

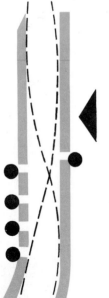

and sounded a lower note than when the tube was open.

If a tube is long enough, a player can make many additional high sounds with it. These are called overtones and sound like the tones you get if you blow a tin whistle too hard and make a sound higher than the one you want. This happens because the column of air in a long, thin tube easily breaks up into halves, thirds, fourths, and even smaller sections. The smaller the section of air is, the higher the pitch it sounds when it vibrates.

When finger holes are closed, full length of tube sounds lowest pitch.

As finger holes are opened, air column shortens and pitches go up.

Finger Holes

If a hole is made in the side of a tube, the pitch of the note it sounds goes up, as if the tube had been cut off at the hole. This happens because the air moves in and out at the hole just as it does at the open end. If a row of holes, which can be opened or closed, is made in a tube, a player can sound many different pitches with the same tube.

A simple finger-hole flute is the Japanese *shakuhachi,* made of bamboo. The player's breath splits against the edge of a notch cut at one end. There are four finger holes on top and a thumb hole beneath.

Bamboo shepherd's pipes, which are still made today, were another early flute. They have a row of six holes along the top. This pipe sounded the seven notes of our do-re-mi scale. To play the lowest note, the player closed all the finger holes. As he opened each finger hole, from the bottom up, he played a higher note.

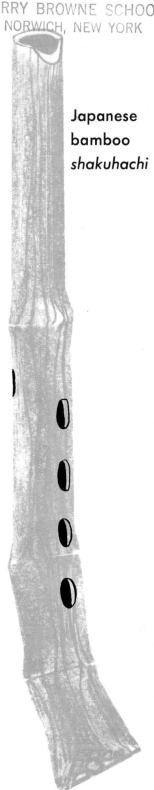

Japanese
bamboo
shakuhachi

11

shepherd's pipe

soprano recorder

alto recorder

Recorders

In the shepherd's pipe there is a plug at the blowing end, which narrows the stream of breath and directs it against the sharp edge of a notch cut into the side of the pipe. From this device grew a group of wooden pipes called recorders, which were popular from the twelfth century to the eighteenth. They were made of hardwood. In the sixteenth century there were seven or eight different sizes of recorders, and they were played as a complete family by themselves. Each instrument had a range of about two octaves, two do-re-mi scales, including the half steps. Recorders have seven finger holes on top and one thumb hole below. Opening the thumb

bass recorder

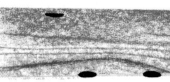

cross section
of tenor recorder

breath
channel

thumb
hole

finger
holes

hole part way or all the way breaks up the air column into shorter sections, so that, with special fingerings, the notes of the upper octave can be sounded.

Bach, Handel, and other composers wrote music especially for the recorder. About the middle of the eighteenth century, however, recorders went out of fashion. Then forty years ago Arnold Dolmetsch began building recorders again. Once more people came to know the joy of this simple instrument.

Usually recorders come in four sizes today. From smallest to largest, they are called soprano, alto, tenor, and bass, as the ranges of singing voices are called.

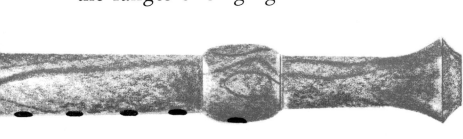

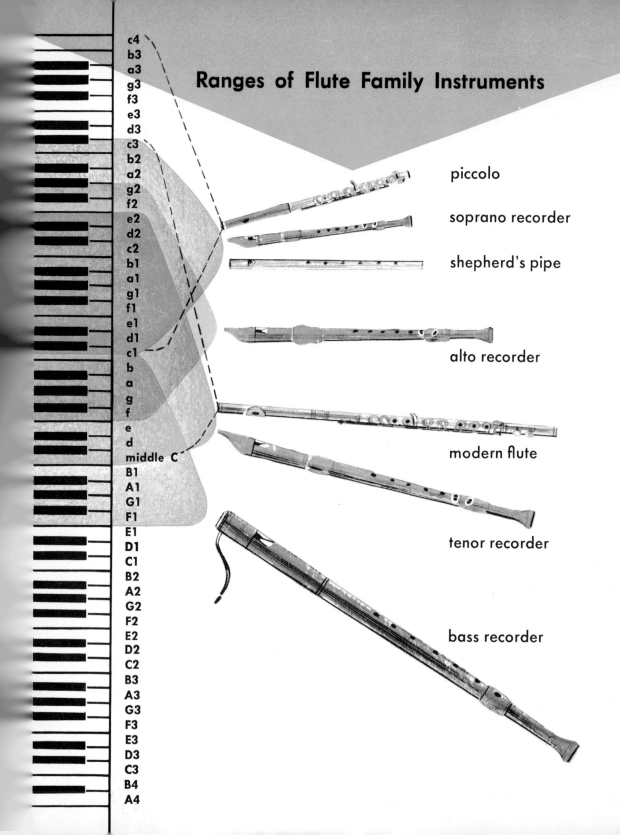

Ranges of Flute Family Instruments

piccolo

soprano recorder

shepherd's pipe

alto recorder

modern flute

tenor recorder

bass recorder

c4
b3
a3
g3
f3
e3
d3
c3
b2
a2
g2
f2
e2
d2
c2
b1
a1
g1
f1
e1
d1
c1
b
a
g
f
e
d
middle C
B1
A1
G1
F1
E1
D1
C1
B2
A2
G2
F2
E2
D2
C2
B3
A3
G3
F3
E3
D3
C3
B4
A4

They actually all play one octave higher than these voices sing, but they seem to sound lower, probably because of their mellow sounds. You can see the actual notes that each recorder plays on the piano keyboard in the diagram on page 14.

The soprano recorder is about twelve inches long and is popular with young people, because it is easy to hold and blow. It only costs six or eight dollars. The pitches it sounds are very high, like those of a piccolo.

The alto recorder is about eighteen inches long. It is the popular melody instrument of the family. Its range is that of high women's and children's voices. The tenor recorder is about twenty-four inches long, twice as long as the soprano recorder, and so it sounds just one octave lower. It plays in the same range as the modern flute. The largest size is the bass recorder—about three feet long. Children

Lower holes on some
recorders are double.
Opening only one of a
pair raises the pitch
a half step.

can sing most of the notes it plays, but its hollow tones seem to be much lower than they really are.

There is much music for recorders—solos, duets, trios, and quartets. In the recording of the Trapp Family singing songs from the musical play, *The Sound of Music,* the sweet clear sound of well-played recorders can be heard. Recorders are good instruments for a beginner to start with, and they are fine enough so that you may enjoy them the rest of your life.

Side-Blown Flutes

Those instruments called flutes today are held sideways. There is a blowing hole at the side near one end instead of the mouth tube built into the shepherd's pipe and recorder. The flute player must make his breath stream narrow and flat himself—there is no mouth tube to do this for him. This makes the flute harder to blow, but gives the player fine control over the sound of his instrument.

At first these flutes had six holes, like the shepherd's pipe, and were made of boxwood. Some of the in-between notes, or half steps, were hard to play in tune on them with only six finger holes, just as they were on the shepherd's pipe. Instead

17

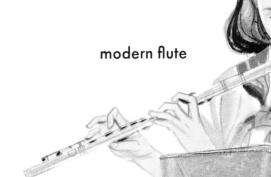

modern flute

of adding another finger hole and a thumb hole, as was done to the recorder, special keys were added to flutes. When a player pressed these keys, they opened additional holes. Otherwise, springs held the keys shut. In this way the flute became a very flexible instrument.

In the nineteenth century a German named Theobald Böhm made more important changes in the flute. He made the finger holes larger and changed the keys to make the fingering easier. He also experimented with brass tubing to find the best inside shape for the flute that would produce a full, even sound. Thus the

six-holed fife

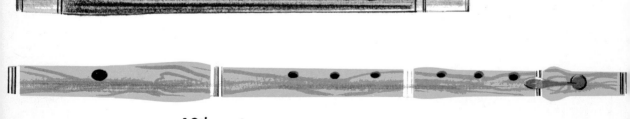

**18th century
one-keyed flute**

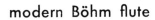
modern Böhm flute

modern piccolo

sound of the shepherd's pipe grew into the sound of the modern flute, on which a solo can be played that will even be heard above the other instruments in the orchestra. The range of the flute is shown on page 14.

The piccolo is a half-sized flute that can play an octave higher than the flute. It is heard in marching bands, and many orchestra composers also call for its sound. A good example of a piccolo solo is the one in *The Stars and Stripes Forever,* the march by John Philip Sousa.

Most modern flutes are made of metal instead of wood, but they still have much the same pure and simple sound.

Making Elderberry Whistles

In many parts of the United States elderberry bushes grow wild. Along country roads and farm fences the woody stalks and flat-looking flower bunches are found. Whistles can be made from the stems of this bush. Cut a few of the thickest stem sections you can find. One section, be-

tween two knots, will be from four to seven inches long. Cut off the longest you have with a coping saw.

Inside an elderberry stem there is soft pith. Push it out with a pencil or any other tool that will fit inside. Next scrape off the bark with your pocketknife. Saw a slit halfway through the stem about an inch from one end. Then whittle at an angle toward the base of the first cut. A small window will appear. Sand the window until the edges are smooth and sharp.

Next find a plug of wood that will just fit into the window end of the tube. A piece of wooden dowel may fit, or the twig of a hardwood tree, such as maple, oak, or

elderberry
flower cluster

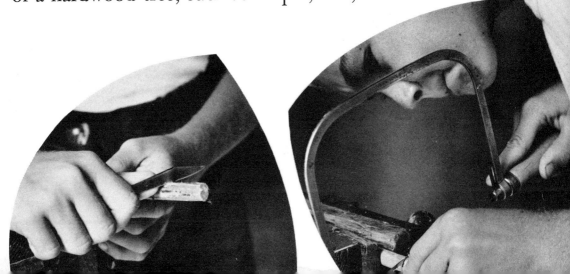

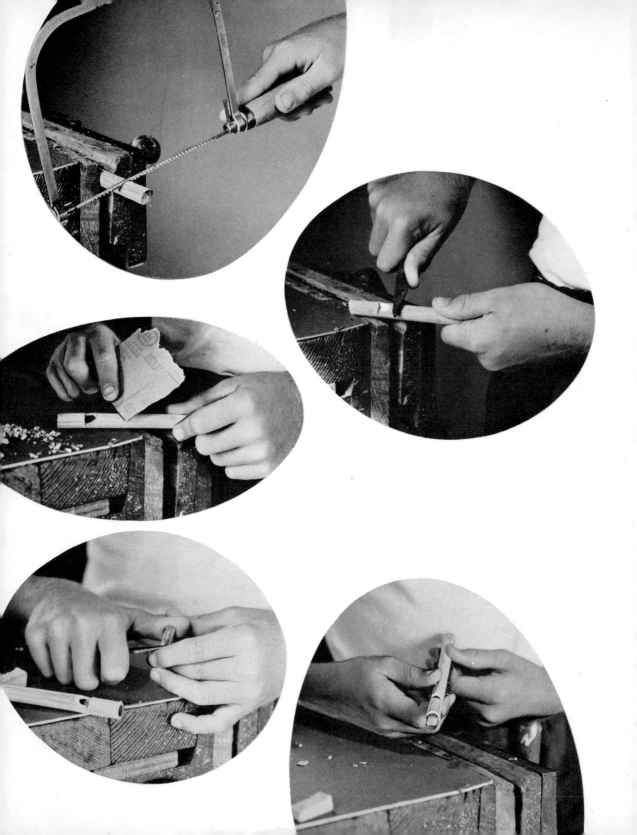

elm. Cut the plug to match the distance from the end of the tube to the window. Sand it or whittle it so that it will go in easily, but stay in place. Tip the plug up on end and slice off about one third of it. Push the plug back into the stem so that the flat side lines up with the window and the end of the plug is even with the end of the tube.

Put your finger over the open end of the stem and blow. If you don't get a good sound, check the window to make sure it is smooth. Look down the plug to see if the breath channel it makes is clear. Push the plug in or out a little, or shave off more of the flat side of the plug. Sometimes the first try will work perfectly. If not, experiment with other stems or plugs until you get a good whistle. You can make several whistles in one afternoon and, if they do not split, they may last for a very long time.

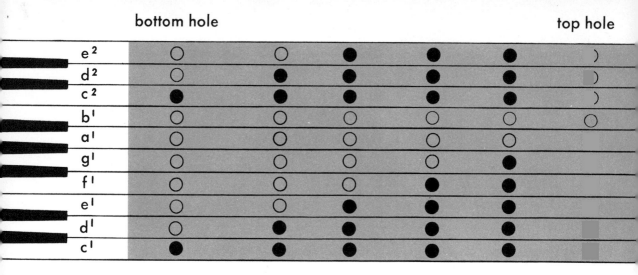

fingering chart   ● = hole closed   ○ = hole open   ◑ = partly open

Making a Shepherd's Pipe

If you can make an elderberry whistle, you can also make a shepherd's pipe. You will need a piece of thin, hollow cane at least 12½ inches long and about ½ inch wide inside. You can order several pieces, so that you have enough to practice on, from the Bamboo and Rattan Works, 901 Jefferson Street, Hoboken, N. J. These

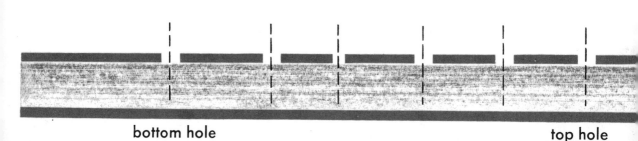

cost only a few cents apiece. You can also use part of a bamboo fishing pole.

Drill through any joints with a wood auger the width of the inside of the cane. Next measure off the points for centers of holes and the crosscut notch for the window. Hold your cane next to the drawing on this page to mark the points. Measure from the window end and leave your tube about ½ inch too long at first.

Clamp the tube in a vise and make the holes about ⅛ inch wide by twisting the point of the small blade of your pocket-knife into the cane. Next saw the cross notch for the window not quite halfway through. Set this end against the work-bench and whittle down toward the notch with a pocketknife. Make the angle as shown in the picture, so that a window

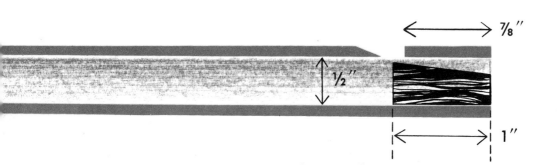

arch appears about ¼ inch long. Round it evenly with the knife and sand it smooth.

Cut or whittle a wooden plug 1 inch long, which will just push into the window end of the tube. Whittle a flat slope on one side. Push in the plug so the narrow part of the breath channel is near the window. See if the pipe will sound. Try it with holes closed and holes open. If there is no clear sound, try pushing the plug in or pulling it out just a bit. Make sure the breath channel is clear. If there is still no sound, whittle a sharper slope on the plug. Everything depends on the plug. If the first doesn't work, make a thicker plug and increase the angle of the flat slope. Be patient; you are making a real instrument.

When you get a clear tone, both with holes open and holes closed, you are ready to tune the notes. When all the holes are tightly closed, the pipe must sound the c^1,

finished
mouth
plug

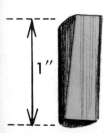

1"

one octave above middle C on the piano. (See the keyboard on page 14.) Close all holes and blow gently. If your tone is below the piano tone, you must shorten the pipe. Saw off only about ⅛ inch at a time until the tone comes up to the right pitch.

The first open hole at the lower end must sound d, the next open hole e, and so on up the white keys of the piano. All the notes will probably be too low at first. To raise a note, widen the hole with a rat-tail file. A wider hole lets more air move in and out and shortens the air column inside the tube more effectively. The third hole may stay smaller than the others, since it only raises the pitch a half step. (There is no black half-step key between e and f on the piano.)

The first three fingers of the right hand cover the lower holes. The first three of the left hand cover the upper holes. To play up the scale, open the holes in order

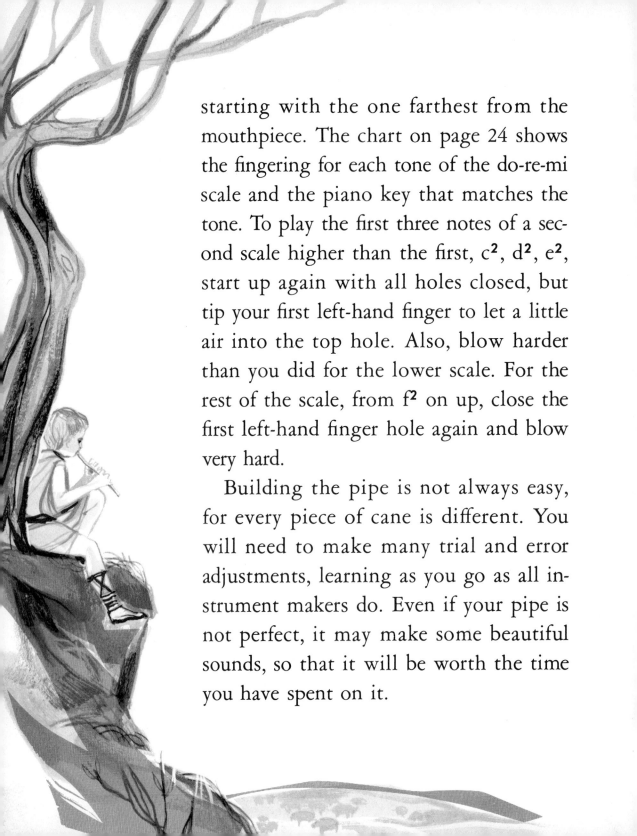

starting with the one farthest from the mouthpiece. The chart on page 24 shows the fingering for each tone of the do-re-mi scale and the piano key that matches the tone. To play the first three notes of a second scale higher than the first, c^2, d^2, e^2, start up again with all holes closed, but tip your first left-hand finger to let a little air into the top hole. Also, blow harder than you did for the lower scale. For the rest of the scale, from f^2 on up, close the first left-hand finger hole again and blow very hard.

Building the pipe is not always easy, for every piece of cane is different. You will need to make many trial and error adjustments, learning as you go as all instrument makers do. Even if your pipe is not perfect, it may make some beautiful sounds, so that it will be worth the time you have spent on it.

Vibrating Reeds

Much as the first flutes came from natural hollow objects, so the simplest reed instruments grow naturally. A shoot of a hollow reed plant, such as green cane, makes a reed instrument. The ends can be pinched flat and scraped thin. These flat, springy pieces are called reeds, after the name of the plant, and the reeds go into the player's mouth.

reed cane for instrument mouth-pieces, drying in the sun

Once the player's breath starts them moving, the reeds tend to swing until they touch. Because of their springiness, they swing apart and keep swinging until they touch again. This happens hundreds of times per second.

The opening and closing of the reeds lets rapid and regular puffs of air into the tube, disturbing the air there and causing it to vibrate. Because the tube is closed much of the time at the reed end, the sound is basically that of a closed pipe. Air

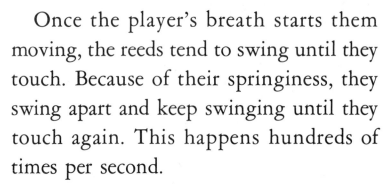

Double reed opens and closes hundreds of times per second.

double reed open

double reed closed

vibrates at the open end, but moves very little at the closed end. This is much the way the closed tube, described on page 8, works.

early Egyptian double reed, and pipe of cane

How the Reed Family Grew

The first reed instruments were actually made of plant stems with finger holes in the sides. When the mouth reeds wore out, the player threw the whole instrument away and made another. Later, to keep from losing a fine instrument, two pieces were used. The reed mouthpiece was pushed into a separate cane tube. When the mouthpiece wore out, only that small section had to be changed.

Some of the oldest reed pipes were played two at a time. This is not as hard as it seems. Put two pinched soda straws in your mouth. You will find you can blow them both at the same time. One straw, without any finger holes, sounds

31

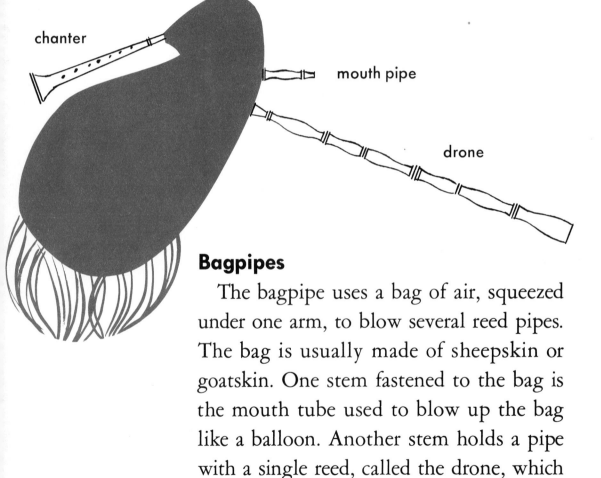

one note while the other, with finger holes, plays a melody at the same time. A player can play a duet with himself, and the straws sound something like a bagpipe.

chanter

mouth pipe

drone

Bagpipes

The bagpipe uses a bag of air, squeezed under one arm, to blow several reed pipes. The bag is usually made of sheepskin or goatskin. One stem fastened to the bag is the mouth tube used to blow up the bag like a balloon. Another stem holds a pipe with a single reed, called the drone, which plays only one sound. A third stem holds the double-reed pipe called the chanter. This pipe has seven finger holes for playing the lively tunes. The chanter is usually cone-shaped. The small part of the cone is near the reed end, inside the bag. This shape makes the sound bright like that of a trumpet, so that it will carry out of doors.

Mouth-Blown Pipes

During the sixteenth century a pipe with a double reed, called the shawm, was popular. Its sound was strong, something like that of the chanter of the bagpipe, but it was blown by mouth. Outdoor bands used shawms of several sizes.

The shawm was too loud to use indoors with softer-sounding instruments. There another pipe with a double reed, called the krummhorn, took its place. This instrument had a mouth cap over the reeds. The narrow tube was made of boxwood, steamed so that the lower end could be

bagpipers
in parade

mouth
cap

double
reed

cross section
of a krummhorn

bent up in a curve. The player blew into the mouth cap, making a pleasant sound like that of an oboe playing softly. The krummhorn has eight holes, like the recorder, but it only plays nine tones. It is good for group music, and was often played with recorders since the different sounds of the two instruments balanced well together. Krummhorns are not common today and must be ordered from special instrument makers. They come in the same four sizes that recorders do, but they sound one octave lower.

In the last half of the seventeenth century a new instrument was added to the reed family. The shawm always sounded loud and did not play high notes very well.

The krummhorn was soft, and its range was limited to nine tones. The new instrument, the oboe, could do many things well, and it became popular quickly. It could play high and low tones smoothly, and it could play soft and loud and in-between. People thought it sounded almost human. The oboe was narrower inside than the shawm, and it had a narrower double reed outside. Today the oboe is one of the modern instruments. It plays solos and plays in the orchestra.

Another modern woodwind instrument played with a double reed is the bassoon. Inside the instrument the tube is bent double so that it contains a long air column and can sound low notes. Since air can move around a corner, a bend in an

modern
oboe

35

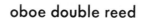

oboe double reed

instrument tube does not affect the pitch. If the bassoon tube were straightened out, it would be about eight feet long. The bassoon plays about the same tones that a man sings. The double reed fits onto a small curved pipe sticking out of the end of the short part of the tube, which is made of wood. The sound is sweet and quaint and very beautiful. The oboe, clarinet, flute, and bassoon form a woodwind quartet, and the bassoon plays the lowest notes of the group.

An extra large bassoon called the contra bassoon, or double bassoon, plays an octave lower. It does not make a very loud sound, but it can play lower than any other instrument in the orchestra.

modern woodwind quartet—
bassoon, oboe, clarinet, and flute

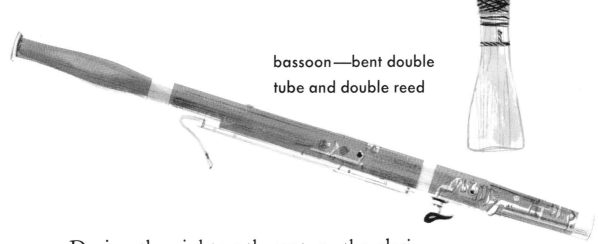

bassoon—bent double
tube and double reed

During the eighteenth century the clarinet was developed in Germany. J. C. Denner, a builder of recorders, made important improvements, and his first clarinet looked like an alto recorder. The clarinet has a single reed. Its high notes are very clear, almost like those of a violin. In fact, it takes the place of violins in concert and marching bands. It has a range of about three octaves. Its low tones have a mellow, hollow sound and are very different from its high tones. In a modern orchestra or band you can hear clarinets of many sizes.

clarinet —
single reed

One of the newest instruments in the reed family is the saxophone. It was invented by Adolphe Sax, in France, in 1846. It is made of a wide, cone-shaped

E♭ clarinet

B♭ clarinet

bass
clarinet

tenor saxophone

brass tube and is played with a single reed like a clarinet. Many clarinet players also play the saxophone. At first it was used in military bands. Then both the saxophone and the clarinet were used in jazz bands. Today the saxophone is the special voice of jazz. The most common sizes are alto, tenor, and baritone. The sound of the tenor saxophone is very human. A jazz player can make it sing, wail, and almost breathe. Now the saxophone is also used sometimes by orchestra composers as well as by jazz players.

As much as they have changed, most of the modern reed instruments still depend for their sound on the slices of living plants, the reeds, which first gave them voice.

Making Willow Reeds

Cut a green willow shoot. It does not need to be more than ¼ inch wide. Pick a smooth section along the shoot about 3 inches long. Run a knife carefully around the bark at each end of this section. Cut or saw away the extra stick at one end.

At the other end split away the bark from the stick. It will make a wooden handle for you to hold. Lay the 3-inch bark section on a post or workbench. Tap the bark gently all around with a stick or knife handle. When it loosens, slide it carefully off the wooden core.

Pinch one end of the bark tube flat. Cut off each corner with your pocketknife. Use the knife to scrape off about ½ inch of the dark green coating of the bark on each

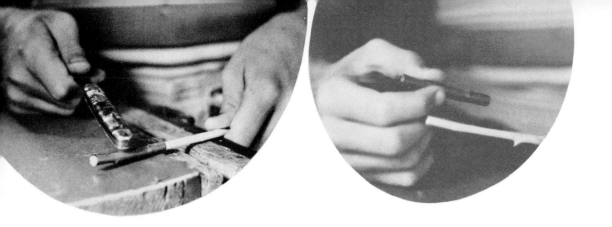

side of the flat end. You now have two thin reeds. Press the tips of the reeds between the pages of a book and pile more books on top. Let the reeds dry for about two hours. When you pull out the pinched end, it will hold some of its flat shape. Spring the reeds apart a bit. Put the reed end well into your mouth so your lips do not touch the reeds. Blow, and you should get a clear, bright tone.

This type of willow double reed was actually used as a mouthpiece on an instrument called a whit horn, which was a cone rolled out of bark. Usually cane is used to make reed instrument mouthpieces today, but the shape of the double reed is about the same.

completed double reed of willow bark

Making a Soda Straw Oboe

As simple as this instrument is to make, when you are finished you will have a true, small double-reed oboe. A soda straw is long enough so that with it you can make an instrument that will sound several pitches. Any paper soda straw can be used. You should have at least a half dozen, so you will be able to waste a few as you learn to make the oboe.

First pinch the straw quite flat at one end. Let it spring back open just a little. Put the pinched end into your mouth as you did the willow reed and blow. If the straw does not sound on the first try, pinch it so that the two flat parts are closer together, or try opening the pinched end a bit more. The straw may make a fine, reedy sound. If not, the reeds may not be free enough.

With scissors cut off each corner of the straw, snipping off very little the first time.

41

Blow and cut, until your straw makes a good sound. You may also need to adjust the pinched end, opening or closing it, at the same time.

As you blow, cut off pieces of the straw with a pair of scissors. The pitch will go up as the straw gets shorter. You can get the same results in another way. Take another straw and cut small holes in it. To cut a hole, pinch the straw, then cut a **V** notch in the flattened part. Make the **V** rather shallow, so that when the straw is pressed back into its normal shape, you can cover the hole tightly with one finger. A straw with an open hole makes the same

sound as a straw that has been cut off at that hole.

If the pinched end of the straw gets very wet, the reeds do not work as well. Keep the pinched end dry and the straw should keep sounding.

Pipe Organs

Although it is not called a woodwind instrument, the great pipe organ combines the voices of the flutes and reeds in a single instrument. One of the first pipe organs, made over 2000 years ago, looked like an overgrown bagpipe. Three bags of animal skin were connected together to a bag filled with air, which was blown through four mouthpieces. Whistle flutes, each a different length so that each sounded a different note, were fastened to the tops of the other three bags. When the bags were filled with air, a plug near the bottom of each whistle flute was pulled

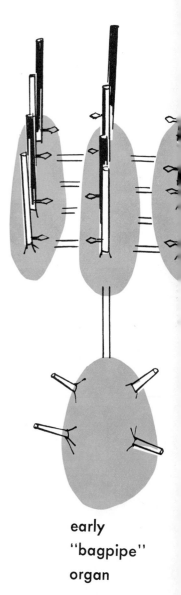

early "bagpipe" organ

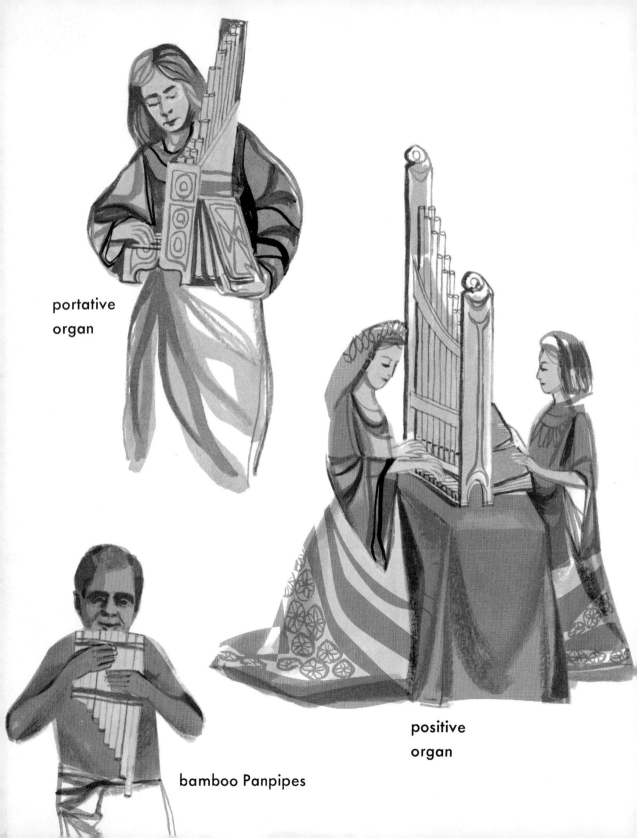

portative
organ

bamboo Panpipes

positive
organ

out to let the air sound the whistle. The rows of whistles looked like the rows of bamboo Panpipes sometimes played by shepherds. The sound might have been something like what you would get from blowing across a row of pop bottles, each filled with more water than the one next to it.

Other early organs had air pumped into them by hand from a bellows, like the kind sometimes used to start a fire in a fireplace. Rows of keys were placed beneath the pipes to open and close them smoothly.

Two small-sized organs were the portative and the positive. The first could be carried by one person as he played. One hand squeezed the bellows for air, and the other hand pressed keys to open the pipes. This organ made a sound like a row of one-note flutes.

The positive organ could also be moved

large wooden organ pipe

reed

organ
flute
pipe

organ
reed
pipe

around, but it had to stay in one place when it was played. One person used two hands on the keys while another worked the bellows at the back.

As organs became larger, they began to be used in churches. At first the music was very simple. It sounded something like what you hear if you play a tune on the piano with two fingers kept three keys apart. Later the melodies began to move in different directions at the same time, and three or even four were played together. The great classical organs built all over Europe were made especially so that these melodies could be heard clearly. The puff of air going suddenly into a pipe started each tone sharply. Pipes with reed vibrators, like the mouthpiece of a clarinet, took turns with the flute pipes or played together with them to make rich combinations. There is no music like the full clear chords of a fine classical organ.

Organ pipes may be as tiny as the length of your fingernail or as big around as a tree and as high as a six-story building. There are as many shapes as there are sizes, each making a special kind of sound. Wide pipes sound hollow, narrow pipes sound sharp or pinched, and cone-shaped pipes have the trumpetlike sound of the bagpipe. Pipes closed at the end have a distant sound, and pipes open at the end sound closer and nearer.

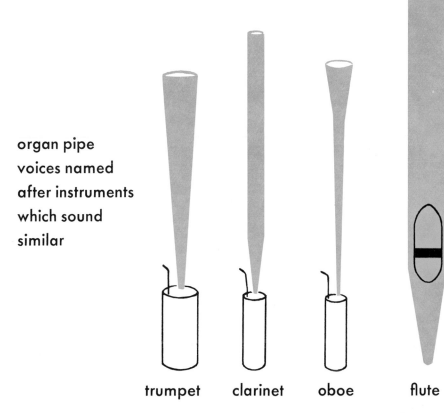

organ pipe
voices named
after instruments
which sound
similar

trumpet   clarinet   oboe   flute

A large organ may have four or five thousand separate pipes, but a fine organ is not the one with the most pipes or the loudest sound. It is the one whose pipe voices sound different and clear, but will balance and combine without losing their special qualities. If you travel, do not miss the chance to hear the fine pipe organs all over the world. If you cannot visit them, you can hear some of them on the fine record called *The Organ,* made by E. Power Biggs. This organist has gone all over the world playing and recording organ sounds. He tells the story of organs and their voices as he plays the music.

Even when listening to the large and powerful organ, do not forget the simple flute and reed pipes, blown by air, which make the wonderful variety of sounds in the group of instruments called the woodwinds.

48